To Kill a Mockingbird Classroom Questions

A SCENE BY SCENE TEACHING GUIDE

Amy Farrell

SCENE BY SCENE
ENNISKERRY, IRELAND

Copyright © 2015 by Amy Farrell.

All rights reserved. No part of this publication may be reproduced, distributed or transmitted in any form or by any means, including photocopying, recording, or other electronic or mechanical methods, without the prior written permission of the publisher, except in the case of brief quotations embodied in critical reviews and certain other noncommercial uses permitted by copyright law. For permission requests, write to the publisher, addressed "Attention: Permissions Coordinator," at the address below.

Scene by Scene
11 Millfield, Enniskerry
Wicklow, Ireland.
www.scenebysceneguides.com

Ordering Information:
Quantity sales. Special discounts are available on quantity purchases by corporations, associations, and others. For details, contact the "Special Sales Department" at the address above.

To Kill a Mockingbird Classroom Questions/Amy Farrell. —1st ed.
ISBN 978-1-910949-00-9

Contents

Chapter One	1
Chapter Two	3
Chapter Three	4
Chapter Four	5
Chapter Five	6
Chapter Six	7
Chapter Seven	8
Chapter Eight	9
Chapter Nine	10
Chapter Ten	11
Chapter Eleven	12
Chapter Twelve	14
Chapter Thirteen	15
Chapter Fourteen	16
Chapter Fifteen	17
Chapter Sixteen	18
Chapter Seventeen	19
Chapter Eighteen	20
Chapter Nineteen	21
Chapter Twenty	22
Chapter Twenty-One	23

Chapter Twenty-Two	24
Chapter Twenty-Three	25
Chapter Twenty-Four	26
Chapter Twenty-Five	27
Chapter Twenty-Six	28
Chapter Twenty-Seven	29
Chapter Twenty-Eight	30
Chapter Twenty-Nine	31
Chapter Thirty	32
Chapter Thirty-One	33
Discussion Questions	34

CLASSROOM QUESTIONS

Chapter One

1. What does the narrator's father, Atticus Finch, work as?

2. What is the town of Maycomb like?

3. Who are the characters in the narrator's family?

4. What is Calpurnia, the cook, like?

5. What details do you learn about the narrator's mother?

6. Describe Dill, the boy who comes to stay next door.

7. Why do the children want to make Boo Radley come out?

8. Describe the Radley place.

9. What do people say about Boo Radley?

10. Why was Mr. Radley's boy not seen for fifteen years?

11. What did Boo Radley do to his father?

12. What description does Jem give of Boo Radley?

13. What do you think of the fact that Boo has been kept in his house for years?

Classroom Questions

Chapter Two

1. Describe Miss Caroline, Scout's teacher.

2. Why does Scout get in trouble with Miss Caroline?

3. Describe Walter Cunningham.

4. Why doesn't Walter take the quarter from the teacher?

5. Describe Scout's personality, from what we've read so far.

Classroom Questions

Chapter Three

1. Why does Jem invite Walter home with them for lunch?

2. Why does Scout get into trouble with Calpurnia?

3. What frightens Miss Caroline after lunch?

4. Describe Burris Ewell.

5. Why doesn't Scout want to go back to school?

6. What kind of man is Mr. Ewell?

CLASSROOM QUESTIONS

Chapter Four

1. What does Scout find in the tree by the Radley place?

2. What does Jem find in the tree?

3. How does Scout end up outside the Radley place?

4. What does 'playing Boo Radley' involve?

5. What does 'being a girl' involve, according to Jem?

Classroom Questions

Chapter Five

1. Describe Miss Maudie.

2. What plan are Jem and Dill working on?

3. What kind of man is Atticus, in your opinion?

CLASSROOM QUESTIONS

Chapter Six

1. What do the boys want to do on Dill's last night?

2. Do you think it's unusual for children to behave like this?

3. What happens when the children are seen?

4. Why does Jem sneak out for his trousers?

Classroom Questions

Chapter Seven

1. How does Scout feel about the second grade?

2. What does Jem tell Scout about 'that night'?

3. What do the children find in the knot-hole of the tree?

4. What reason did Mr. Nathan give for filling the hole in the tree? Do you believe this was his real reason?

5. Describe Jem, based on what we know of him so far.

CLASSROOM QUESTIONS

Chapter Eight

1. Why does Scout think the world is ending one morning?

2. How do the children make a snowman?

3. Why is Scout woken up in the middle of the night?

4. What gives Scout a fright?

5. How does Miss Maudie react to her loss?

CLASSROOM QUESTIONS

Chapter Nine

1. What makes Scout want to fight Cecil Jacobs?

2. What reason does Atticus give Scout for defending Tom Robinson?

3. Describe Uncle Jack.

4. Does Scout enjoy spending time with Francis?

5. What problem does Aunt Alexandra have with Scout?

6. Why does Scout fight with Francis? Do you blame her?

7. Why does Scout think her uncle isn't fair?

8. What is Atticus worried about as the chapter ends?

Classroom Questions

Chapter Ten

1. Why does Scout call her father "feeble"?

2. Why is it a sin to kill a mockingbird?

3. What's wrong with the dog, Tim Johnson?

4. How is the dog behaving?

5. What does Atticus do that impresses his children?

6. How do you know Jem looks up to his father?

CLASSROOM QUESTIONS

Chapter Eleven

1. Describe Mrs. Dubose.

2. Why does Scout hate her?

3. Why is Atticus so polite to Mrs. Dubose?

4. What does Jem do to Mrs. Dubose's camellia bushes and why does he do this?

5. Why doesn't Atticus go along with what everyone else thinks?

6. What does Jem have to do for Mrs. Dubose as punishment for destroying her camellias?

7. Scout says Mrs. Dubose was horrible. What did she look like?

8. What was the cause of Mrs. Dubose's fits, according to Atticus?

9. Why does Atticus call Mrs. Dubose a "great lady"?

10. Do you think she was a brave woman?

Classroom Questions

Chapter Twelve

1. Why doesn't Dill arrive at the start of the summer?

2. In what ways is Jem changing?

3. How do the people in Calpurnia's church react when they see the children?

4. Who is the church collection for?

5. What has Tom Robinson been accused of?

6. What does Scout realise about Calpurnia?

Classroom Questions

Chapter Thirteen

1. Why has Aunt Alexandra come to stay?

2. What does Aunt Alexandra consider to be important about people?

CLASSROOM QUESTIONS

Chapter Fourteen

1. What do Atticus and Aunt Alexandra argue about?

2. Why does Scout fight with Jem?

3. How does Atticus react to the children's discovery of Dill? What does this tell you about Atticus?

4. What reason does Dill give for running away?

5. What kind of father is Atticus, in your opinion?

CLASSROOM QUESTIONS

Chapter Fifteen

1. Why does Mr. Heck Tate visit Atticus?

2. Why does Aunt Alexandra think Atticus is disgracing the family?

3. Why is Jem scared?

4. Where does Atticus go on Sunday night?

5. Describe the men that arrive.

6. Why have they come here?

7. How do they react to Scout's conversation with Mr. Cunningham?

Classroom Questions

Chapter Sixteen

1. What do Atticus and Alexandra disagree about at breakfast?

2. Atticus tells his children, "Mr Cunningham was part of a mob last night, but he was still a man." What does this mean?

3. Why have so many people come to town?

4. What information does Jem provide about Mr. Dolphus Raymond?

5. "The court appointed Atticus to defend him. Atticus aimed to defend him. That's what they didn't like about it." Explain what these lines mean.

CLASSROOM QUESTIONS

Chapter Seventeen

1. What information does Mr. Heck Tate give as evidence?

2. What injuries did Mayella have?

3. Describe the Ewell family, based on the information Scout gives us.

4. What kind of man is Bob Ewell, in your opinion?

5. What does Bob Ewell announce in evidence, that causes a stir in the courtroom?

6. Do you think Bob Ewell cares about his daughter, Mayella? Explain your answer.

7. What point does Atticus try to make, about the lack of a doctor being called on the night in question?

8. Why does Atticus ask Bob Ewell to sign his name?

CLASSROOM QUESTIONS

Chapter Eighteen

1. What reason does Mayella give for Tom Robinson being in her yard that night?

2. What does she say happened?

3. Why does Mayella think Atticus is making fun of her? What does this tell you about her?

4. What kind of life has Mayella?
   Do you feel sorry for her?

5. Is Atticus a good lawyer, in your opinion?

6. Why does Tom Robinson look "oddly off balance"?

7. Do you believe Mayella's testimony?

CLASSROOM QUESTIONS

Chapter Nineteen

1. What does Tom Robinson reveal about how well he knew Mayella?

2. What makes Mayella so lonely, in Scout's opinion?

3. What does Tom say happened on November twenty-first of the previous year?

4. What kind of man is Tom Robinson, in your opinion?

5. Why did Tom run away?

6. 'You felt sorry for her, you felt sorry for her?' Explain Mr. Gilmer's attitude in this line.

7. What makes Dill start crying?

CLASSROOM QUESTIONS

Chapter Twenty

1. Why does Mr. Dolphus Raymond pretend to be drunk all the time? What does this tell you about the attitudes of the people of Maycomb?

2. What opinion does Mr. Dolphus Raymond have of Atticus?

3. Why does Atticus feel "this case should never have come to trial"?

4. What does Atticus say Mayella is guilty of?

5. Do you find Atticus' closing speech to the jury convincing?

CLASSROOM QUESTIONS

Chapter Twenty-One

1. Why has Calpurnia arrived at the courthouse?

2. Do you agree that the trial was no place for children?

3. What makes Jem so confident that their side will win?

4. What does Scout take as a bad sign as the jury return?

5. What is your reaction to the verdict?

6. Why do the people in the balcony stand up as Atticus passes?

CLASSROOM QUESTIONS

Chapter Twenty-Two

1. How do the family react to the verdict?

2. Why is food left on their back porch?

3. What does Miss Maudie want to tell the children?

4. What do the children hear Bob Ewell did to Atticus?

CLASSROOM QUESTIONS

Chapter Twenty-Three

1. How did Atticus react to Bob Ewell? What does this tell you about him?

2. Where is Tom Robinson being kept at this stage?

3. What point does Atticus make about racism in the courts?

4. What view does Aunt Alexandra have of the Cunninghams?

5. What different opinions do the children have on "different kinds of folks"?

Classroom Questions

Chapter Twenty-Four

1. How do the ladies of Alexandra's missionary circle treat Scout?

2. Are these ladies Christian in their attitudes?

3. Why does Miss Maudie ask, "His food doesn't stick going down, does it?"

4. Why does Atticus need to go out to Helen Robinson's house?

CLASSROOM QUESTIONS

Chapter Twenty-Five

1. How did Helen react to seeing Atticus at her home?

2. "To Maycomb, Tom's death was typical." Explain this line.

3. What does Mr. Underwood write about in the paper?

4. What do you think about the way the people of Maycomb treated Tom and his family?

Classroom Questions

Chapter Twenty-Six

1. What changes in the children's routines when they return to school this year?

2. According to Miss Gates, what is the difference between America and Germany?

3. What problem does Scout have with Miss Gates and what she says about persecution?

4. How does Jem react when Scout mentions Tom Robinson's case? What does this tell you?

CLASSROOM QUESTIONS

Chapter Twenty-Seven

1. What happens to Judge Taylor?

2. What does Mr. Link Deas do for Helen?
   What kind of man does this make him, in your opinion?

3. Why does Atticus think Bob Ewell bears everyone to do with the case a grudge?

4. What is planned for Halloween?

5. What part will Scout play in the pageant?
   What does her costume involve?

Classroom Questions

Chapter Twenty-Eight

1. What goes wrong for Scout in the pageant? How would you feel if you were her?

2. How does Mrs. Merriweather react to Scout's mistake?

3. What does Jem notice as the children walk home?

4. What happens to the children as they walk home?

5. Describe Jem's injuries.

6. What shocking information does Heck Tate give Atticus?

CLASSROOM QUESTIONS

Chapter Twenty-Nine

1. Why does Heck Tate think Scout's costume saved her life?

2. Describe the man who saved the children.

CLASSROOM QUESTIONS

Chapter Thirty

1. Why does Atticus object to things being "hushed up"?

2. Why does Heck Tate insist that Bob Ewell fell on his own knife?

3. Who is Heck Tate protecting?

Classroom Questions

Chapter Thirty-One

1. What details does Scout notice about Boo?

2. Why doesn't Scout "lead him home"?

3. Why is Scout sad as she heads home?

4. What does Scout imagine on the Radley porch? Why does she do this?

5. Do you like how the story ends? Explain why.

CLASSROOM QUESTIONS

Discussion Questions

1. Is Atticus Finch a good man? Explain.

2. Do you think the children have suffered because they had no mother? Explain.

3. How does the guilty verdict in Tom Robinson's case make you feel?

4. Is loneliness a theme in this novel? Explain.

5. What point does this novel make about bravery? Explain.

6. Why do you think this story is told from Scout's point of view? Explain.

7. What kind of life has Boo Radley?

8. How are black people treated in Maycomb?

Scene by Scene

Scene by Scene guides are written by teachers, for teachers. This guide forms the basis of her lessons when teaching the text it accompanies. The aim of this guide is to be a time-saving resource, helping busy teachers to prepare classes and set homework. We hope this guide leads to enjoyable lessons and rewarding classroom experiences, for teachers and students alike.

About the author

This guide's author, Amy Farrell, is a secondary school English teacher from Co. Wicklow, teaching in north County Dublin since 2004.

SCENE BY SCENE TEACHING GUIDES

Scene by Scene Series

Hamlet Scene by Scene

King Lear Scene by Scene

Macbeth Scene by Scene

Romeo and Juliet Scene by Scene

Shakespeare Scene by Scene Volume 1

Classroom Questions Series

A Doll's House Scene by Scene

Animal Farm Classroom Questions

Foster Classroom Questions

WWW.SCENEBYSCENEGUIDES.COM

Good Night, Mr. Tom Classroom Questions

Martyn Pig Classroom Questions

Of Mice and Men Scene by Scene

Pride and Prejudice Classroom Questions

Private Peaceful Classroom Questions

The Fault in Our Stars Classroom Questions

The Old Man and the Sea Classroom Questions

The Outsiders Classroom Questions

To Kill a Mockingbird Classroom Questions

The Spinng Heart Classroom Questions

Visit www.scenebysceneguides.com to find out more about Scene by Scene teaching guides and workbooks.

www.ingramcontent.com/pod-product-compliance
Lightning Source LLC
Chambersburg PA
CBHW071039080526
44587CB00015B/2690